Consecration to Mary
for Little Ones

Written by Kimberly Fries

Illustrated by Sue Kouma Johnson

Copyright © 2019 Kimberly Fries. All rights reserved.

www.mylittlenazareth.com

My Little
NAZARETH
BRINGING CHRIST INTO THE HOME

No part of this book may be reproduced by any means without the written permission of the author.

First Edition: January 2019

ISBN-13: 9781793135209

This book is dedicated to Our Lady.
May many little ones be brought to her through this book.

And to the great saints who have worked tirelessly
to spread devotion to the Immaculata.
To Jesus through Mary!

*Let us run to Mary, and, as her little children,
cast ourselves into her arms with a perfect confidence.
– St. Francis de Sales*

A NOTE TO PARENTS

As our children begin to know, love, and serve God, helping them to prepare to consecrate themselves to Mary can be a great gift to them. The word consecrate ultimately means to declare sacred. As parents, we can guide our children to recognize their sacredness and special mission from God. In addition, we can teach our children that from little on, Mary is by their side and helping them to become holy.

Daily Prayers: The prayers at the bottom of each page are simply a guideline. Feel free to add daily prayers, such as praying a series of Hail Marys or a family Rosary.

Consecration Date: On the following page there is a list of Marian feast days. With your child, choose one of the feasts and then begin Day 1 of this book on the starting date of that feast. This feast will be a very important date for your child; one that can be celebrated every year.

Consecration Dates

Marian Feast Day	Starting Date	Consecration Date
Our Lady of Lourdes	January 9	February 11
Annunciation	February 20*	March 25
Our Lady of Fatima	April 10	May 13
Visitation	April 28	May 31
Immaculate Heart of Mary	Mon. of the 4th Week of Easter	Sat. following the 2nd Sunday after Pentecost
Our Lady of Mt. Carmel	June 13	July 16
Assumption	July 13	August 15
Queenship of Mary	July 20	August 22
Nativity of Mary	August 6	September 8
Holy Name of Mary	August 10	September 12
Our Lady of Sorrows	August 13	September 15
Our Lady of the Rosary	September 4	October 7
Presentation of Mary	October 19	November 21
Immaculate Conception	November 5	December 8
Our Lady of Guadalupe	November 9	December 12
Mary, Mother of God	November 29	January 1
Presentation of the Lord	December 31	February 2

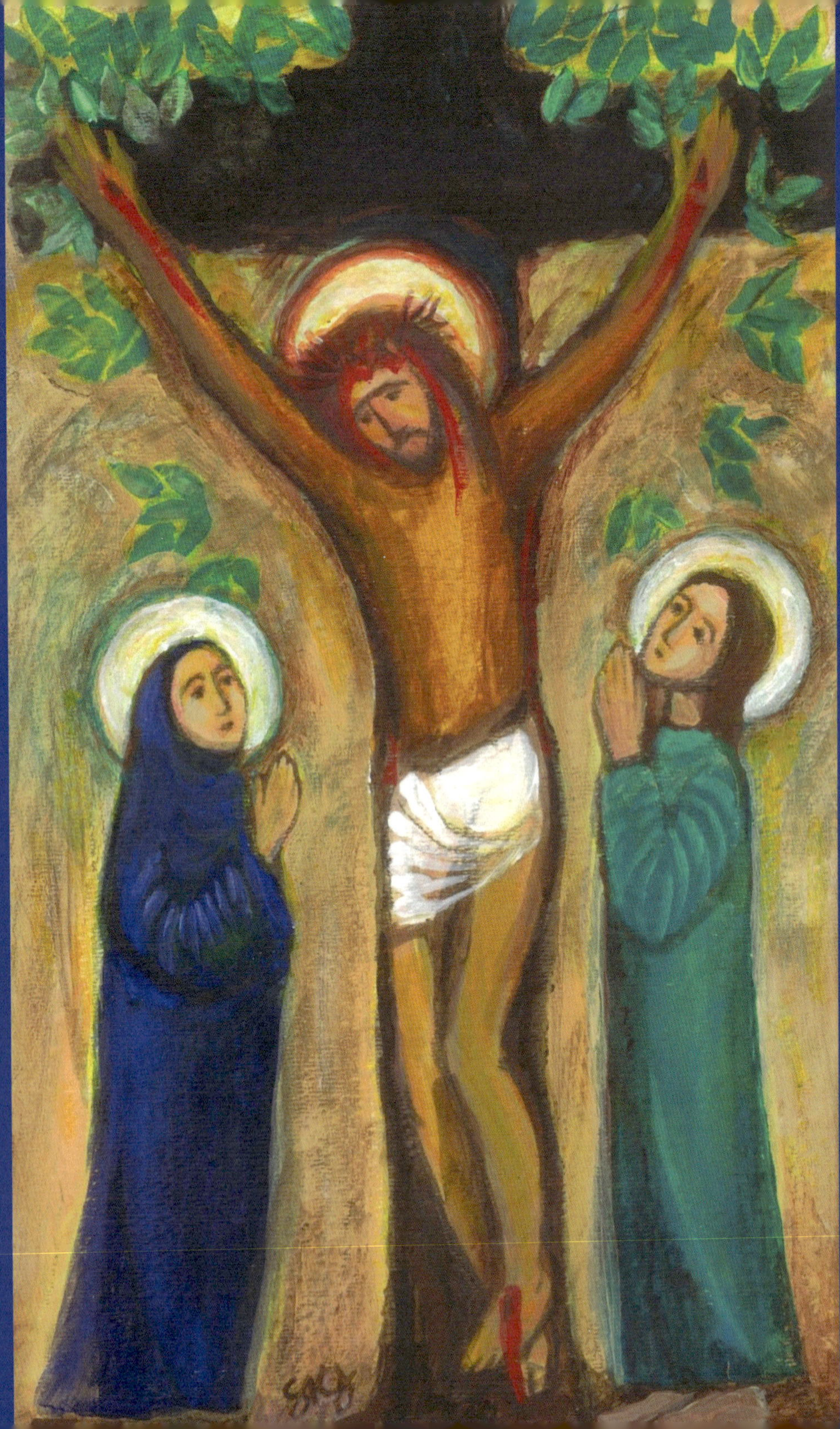

DAY 1

Behold your mother. – John 19:27

Did you know that there is a queen in heaven who has a special mission for you? Her name is Mary. She is not only a queen. She is also the Mother of God and your mother, too. You are going to learn all about Mary in this book. You will also learn about the special mission she has given you. Be sure to pay close attention and open your heart to the love of your heavenly queen.

Prayer: Mary, I am so glad you are my mother in heaven!

DAY 2

And Mary said, "My soul magnifies the Lord."
— Luke 1:46-55

What do you know about this heavenly queen? Mary gave birth to Jesus in Bethlehem, raised him when he was a boy, and suffered beside him as he was dying on the cross at Calvary. God gave Mary a wonderful and very special mission. God gave Mary the mission of being the mother of Jesus, Christ the King.

Prayer: Mary, thank you for being Jesus' mother!

Day 3

I am the Immaculate Conception.
- Our Lady of Lourdes

In order for Mary to fulfill her mission of bringing Jesus to us, God made Mary the Immaculate Conception. This means that when God created Mary, she did not have any sin on her soul. She also never sinned throughout her life on earth. This way Jesus could come to earth through Mary, so pure and sinless.

Prayer: Mary, I am so happy that you are the Immaculate Conception!

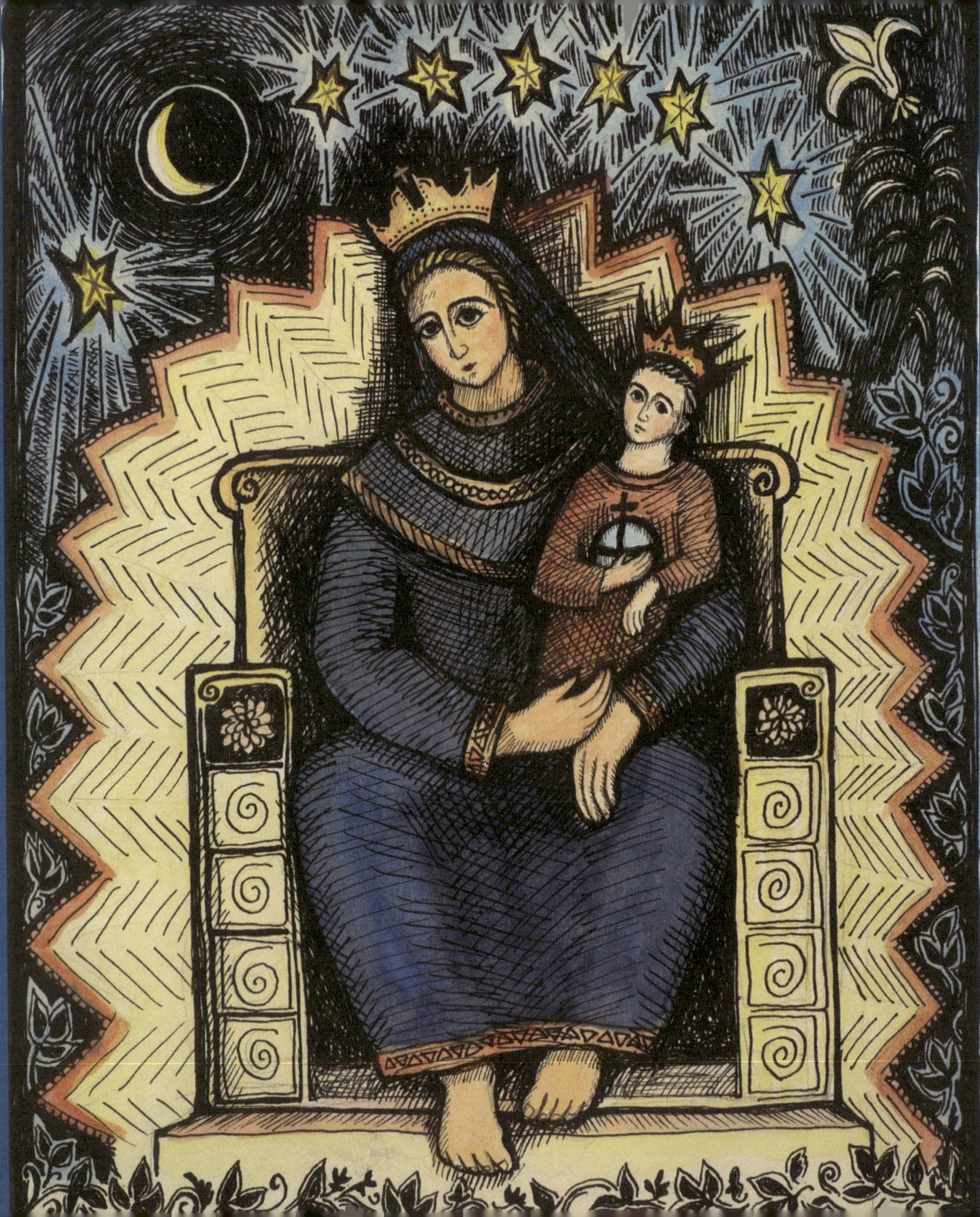

Day 4

God the Father gathered all the waters together and called them the seas (Maria in Latin). He gathered all his graces together and called them Mary. – St. Louis de Montfort

God did not need to create Mary. He could have sent Jesus a different way, using a different plan. But he decided to use Mary, a simple young girl, to bring God into the world. In Mary, pure and holy, our savior entered this world. Mary simply replied, "Be it done unto me according to thy word!"

Prayer: Mary, I am so happy God chose you to bring Jesus into the world!

DAY 5

The Son of God became man for our salvation but only in Mary and through Mary. — St. Louis de Montfort

God's plans are always amazing. They are more beautiful than you can imagine. God's plan for Mary is just that: remarkable! Why would God choose to use a young girl to send the Son of God into this world? Maybe he chose her to show the power of God. Maybe he chose Mary so you can see how a young girl or boy can do great things for God.

Prayer: Mary, I am so glad that God chose you!

DAY 6

We saw... a lady dressed in white...
more brilliant than the sun. – St. Lucia

With such a special mission from God, can you imagine how beautiful Mary must be? Close your eyes and picture Mary in your mind and heart. What is she wearing? Is she saying anything to you? Would you like to tell her anything? Mary loves talking with you, her child. She wants you to imagine that she is right beside you.

Prayer: Mary, speak to me in my heart!

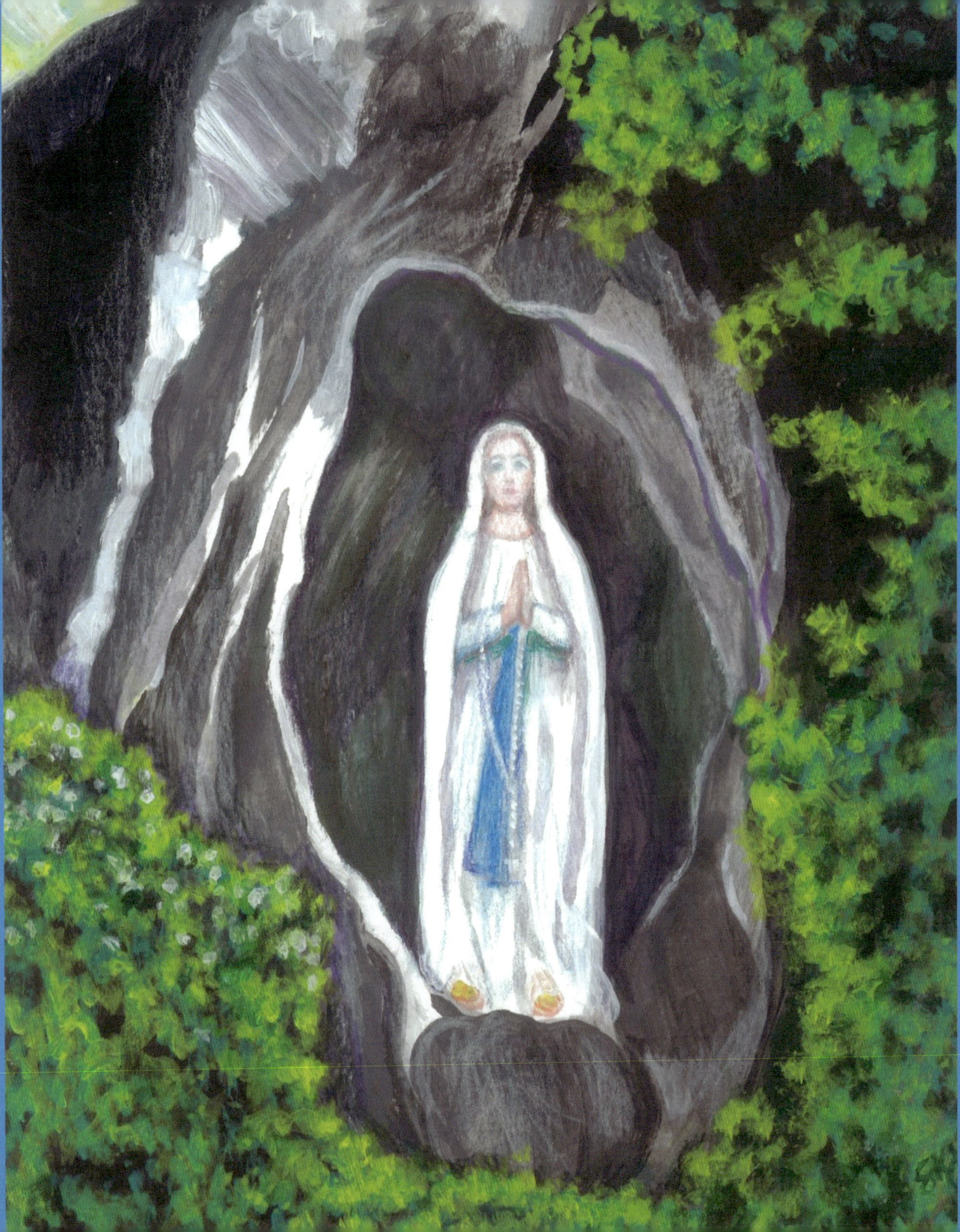

Day 7

Mary, Mother of Jesus, please be a mother to me now.
— St. Teresa of Calcutta

When should you talk to Mary? Anytime! Tell her when something really wonderful happens, like when you have lots of fun playing with your friends or you get a special gift. Ask Mary to be with you when you are really sick or feel especially sad. Call upon your mother in heaven whenever you would like. She loves you and is always praying for you.

Prayer: Mary, help me to remember to pray to you!

DAY 8

Let us live as the Blessed Virgin lived... loving God only, trying to please God only in all that we do.
— St. John Vianney

You can learn so much from Mary, who showed us how to live holy lives. She was obedient by always following God's commandments. Mary was patient when waiting for Jesus to arrive. She was also very loving to her husband and son. God is calling you to be good and live a holy life, too. How can you act more like Mary? How would she act at home, at school, or at Mass?

Prayer: Mary, help me to live a holy life!

Day 9

She is more Mother than Queen. — St. Therese

Though Mary is the beautiful Queen of Heaven and Earth, more than anything she loves being Jesus' mother and your mother, too. She loves to see you grow, learn, play, and laugh. Mother Mary is always praying to her Son for you. She wants you to grow up strong and healthy. Most importantly, she wants you to love God very much, so that you can become a saint in heaven with her forever.

Prayer: Mary, help me to grow up strong and holy!

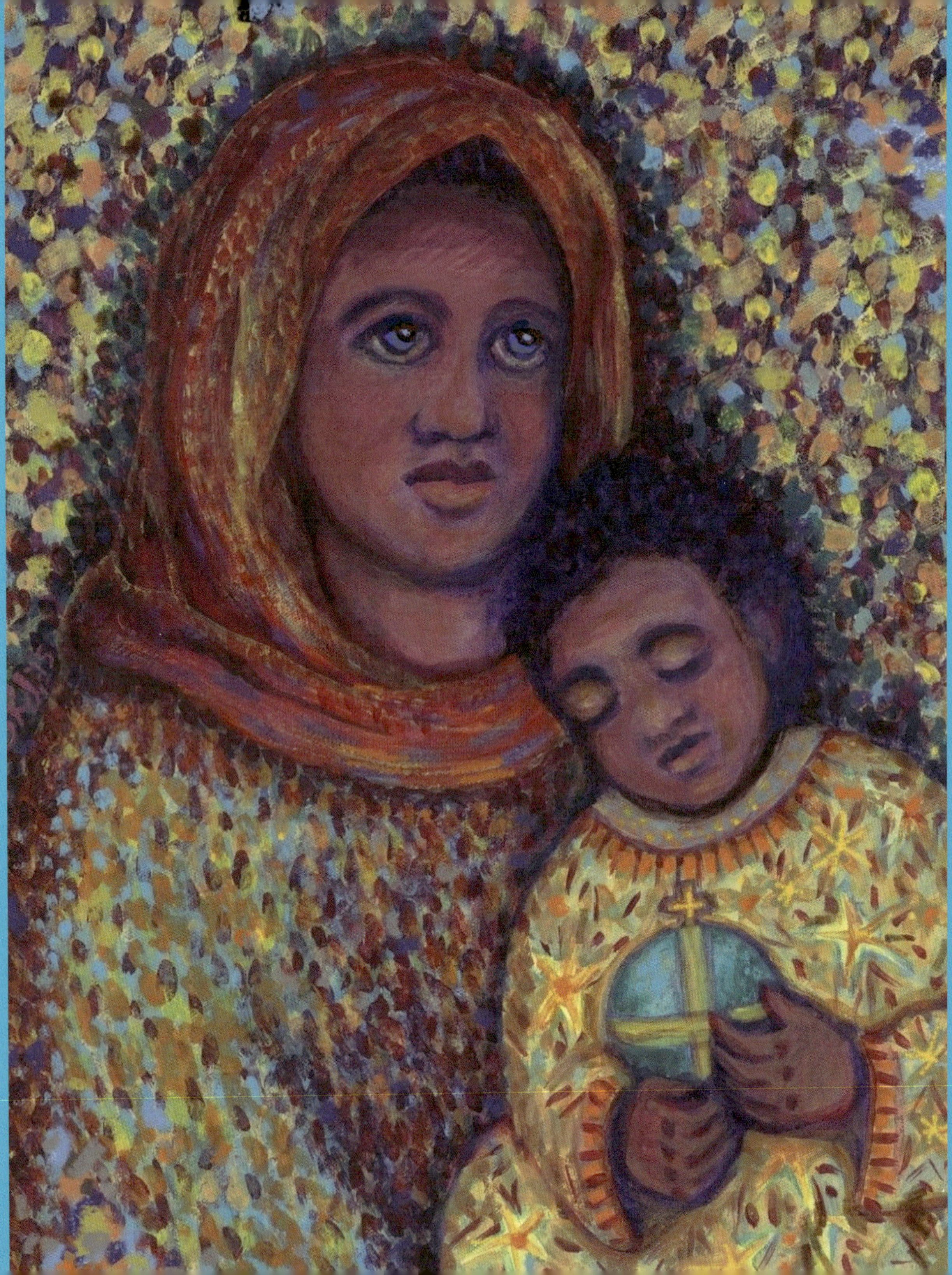

DAY 10

Give yourself up into the arms of your Heavenly Mother. She will take good care of your soul. — St. Pio of Pietrelcina

When Jesus was a baby, Mary took care of him all day and night. She was a very good mother to him. She fed him and taught him. Just as she took good care of Jesus, she will take good care of you. If you are scared or alone, talk to her and she will comfort you. If you are sick or unhappy, she will be right by your side. Always remember that Mary is there and you will have peace.

Prayer: Mary, thank you for being my mother!

DAY 11

*If you are in danger, if your hearts are confused, turn to Mary.
She is our comfort, our help, turn towards her and you will be saved.*
– St. Frances Xavier Cabrini

Since Mary is your Mother, she understands that, though you want to be good, sometimes you choose to act selfishly. She wants you to go to her then, too, so that she can offer you love and support. She will always be right at your side, just as a mother comforts her child.

Prayer: Mary, I want to go to you,
even when I'm acting selfishly.

DAY 12

*As in the first garden Eve brought destruction,
so in the garden of her womb, Mary would now bring Redemption.
– Ven. Fulton Sheen*

Do you know the story of Adam and Eve? They were the first man and woman created by God. Although they loved God, they were tempted to disobey God. When they did disobey him, sin came into the world. But then God sent Jesus, the new Adam, and Mary, the New Eve. Jesus and Mary teach us how to obey and trust God.

Prayer: Mary, the new Eve, help me to obey and trust God!

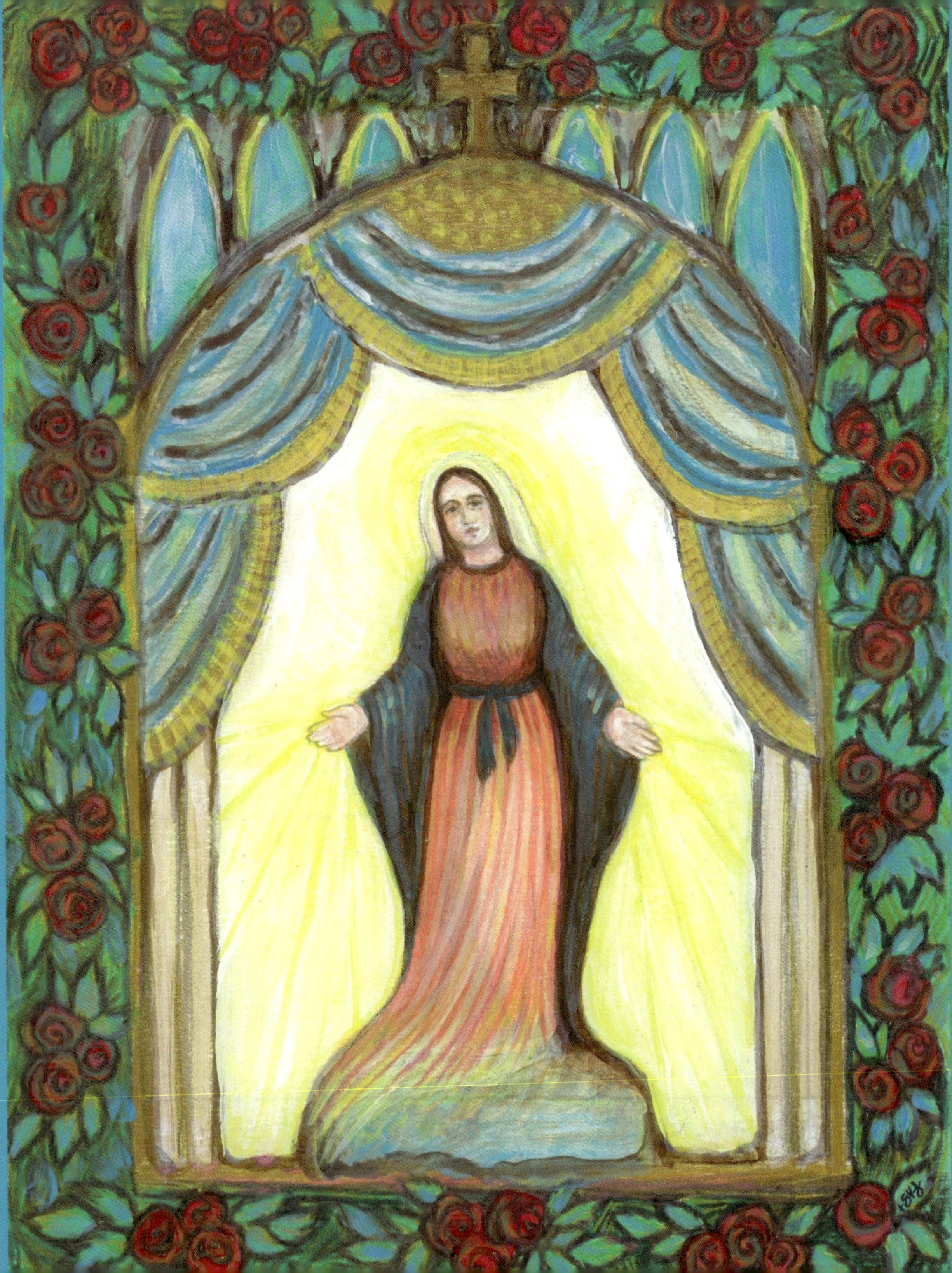

DAY 13

Never be afraid of loving the Blessed Virgin too much. You can never love her more than Jesus did.
– St. Maximilian Kolbe

I hope you are falling more in love with Mary as you learn about her. But do you know who loves Mary more than you? Her own Son, Jesus. He is so happy that you are learning about his mother. Close your eyes and ask Jesus how much he loves Mary. Then tell him how much you love his mother.

Prayer: Mary, Jesus loves you so much!

Day 14

Mary is the safest, easiest, shortest, and most perfect way of approaching Jesus. — St. Louis de Montfort

Because Mary is Jesus' mother, she knows him very well. If you want to know Jesus well, too, you can talk to Mary about him. She will teach us about her son and his life on earth. Mary helps us to love him very much. She will also pray to Jesus for us. Her prayers are very powerful since she is the Mother of God and Queen of Heaven.

Prayer: Mary, I want to always stay close to you!

Day 15

Those who have great devotion to Mary not only will be saved but also will, through her intercession, become great saints. Furthermore, their holiness will grow from day to day.
— St. Vincent Palotti

Every day that you spend with Mary you will become closer to Jesus. She encourages you to always do God's will. Once at a wedding feast, Mary told the servants, "Do whatever he tells you." Then Jesus told them to bring him water, which he turned into wine! If you listen to Jesus and do what he tells you, he will work miracles.

Prayer: Mary, help me to do whatever Jesus tells me!

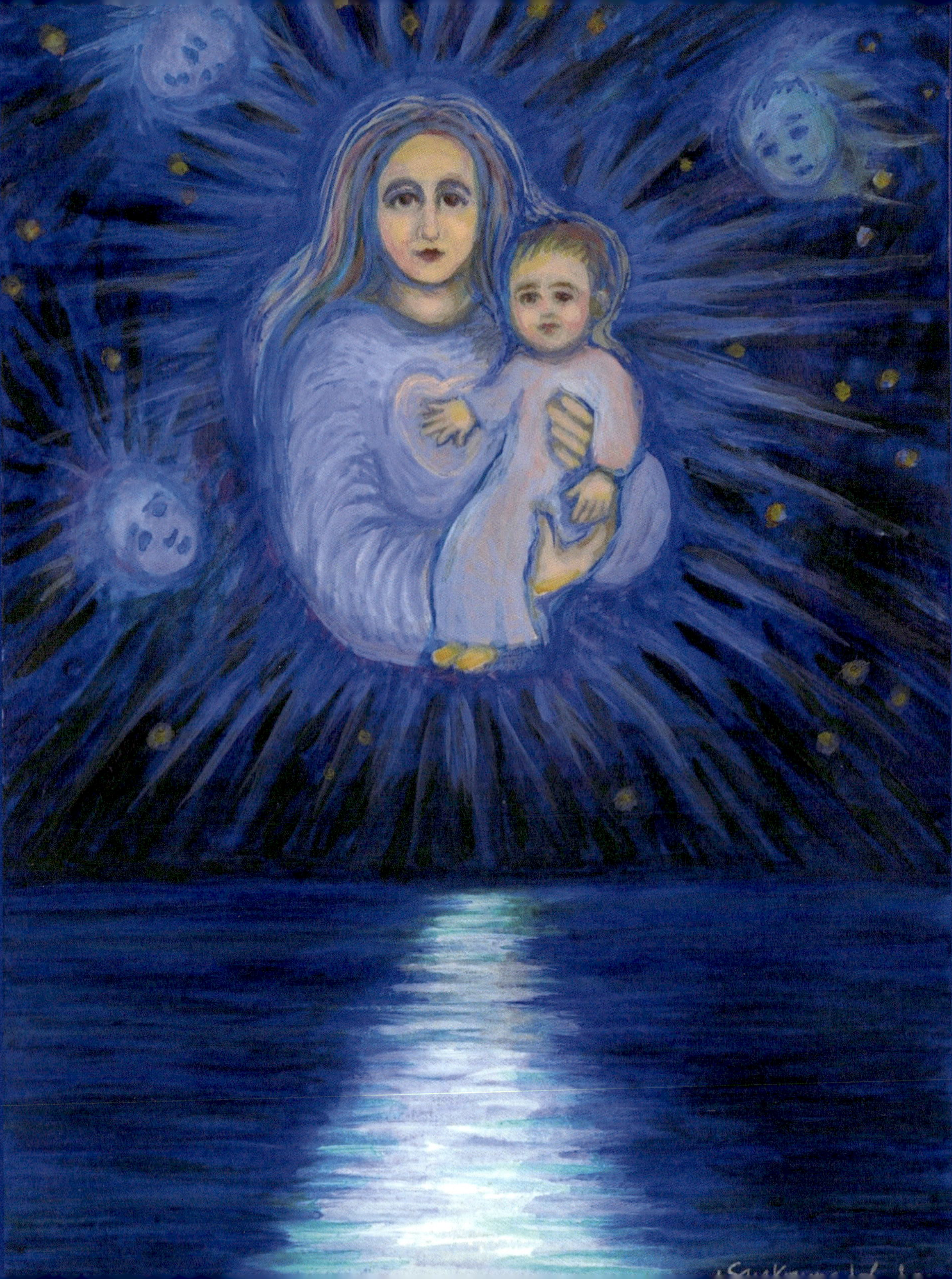

Day 16

Before, by yourselves, you couldn't. Now, you have turned to our Lady, and with her, how easy! – St. Josemaria Escriva

Sometimes you might feel like you are too small to do great things for God. But this is not true at all. Mary's life shows that God can do mighty things through someone who is very humble and little. Many children like you have done great things. You are meant for greatness! You have a important and powerful mission from Mary!

Prayer: Mary, I know I am little, but I want a great mission!

DAY 17

What a joy to remember that she is our Mother! Since she loves us and knows our weakness, what have we to fear?
– St. Therese

What if you think that you cannot handle a great mission? What if you make mistakes? Do not worry, Mary, your mother, will help and guide you. She already knows all of your weaknesses and will be there for you if you fall. As a child of Mary, you have nothing to fear with her by your side.

Prayer: Mary, I am not afraid of anything with you by my side!

DAY 18

Pray, my children. God will answer before long. My Son lets Himself be moved. - Our Lady of Pontmain

In order to grow in holiness, you must be very close to God. Mary wants you to pray to God often throughout each day. Tell God all about your day, the good and the bad. But, also listen to God. You can listen to him with your heart. He will speak to you in your heart, and Mary will speak to you, as well. They will teach you how to be holy.

Prayer: Mary, remind me to pray to God every day!

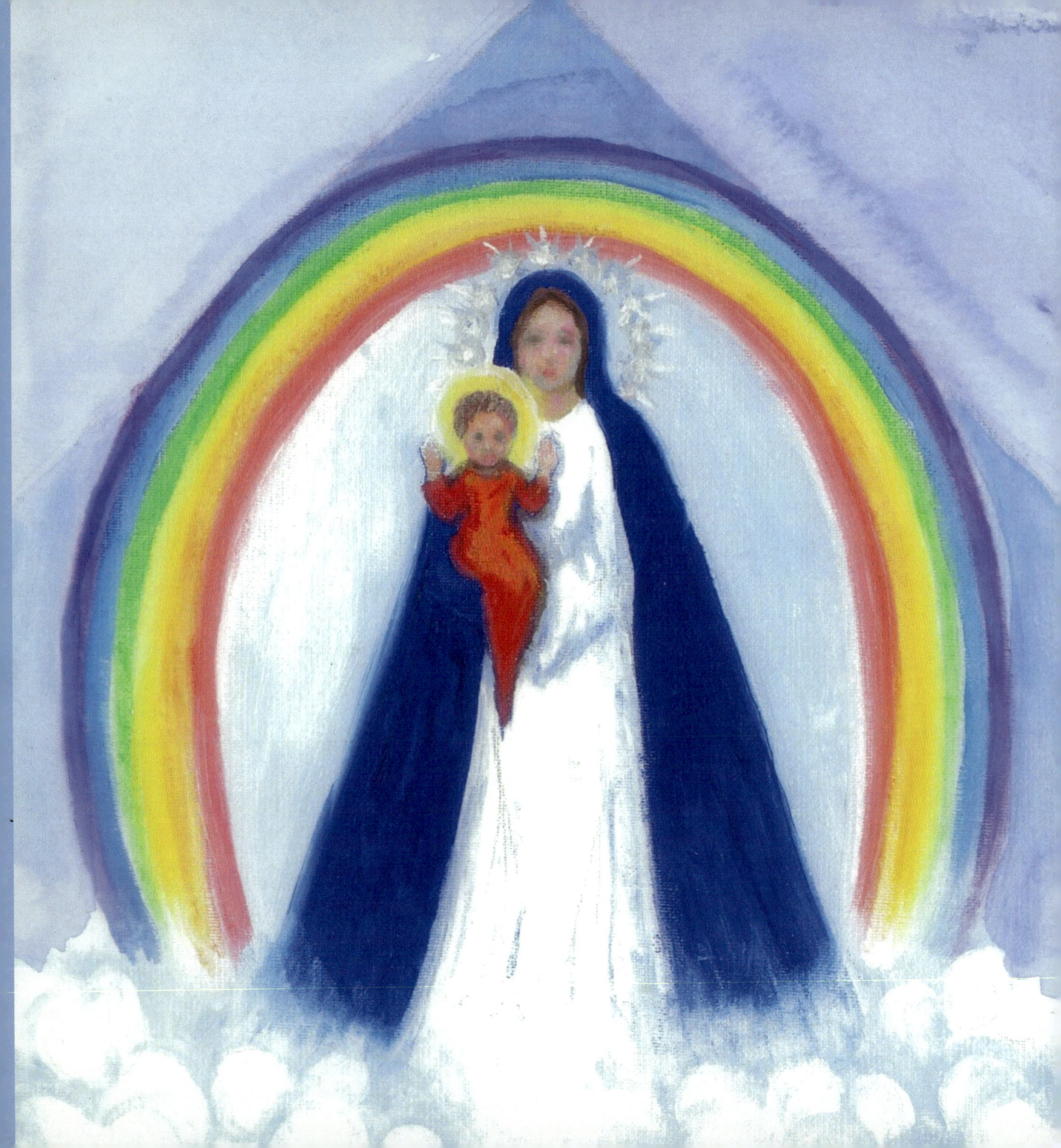

DAY 19

When the Holy Spirit finds Mary in a soul, He flies to it.
– St. Louis de Montfort

When God sent Jesus to Mary and made her the Mother of God, the Holy Spirit came to her. Since then, the Holy Spirit has never left her. When you pray to Mary and take her as your mother, you will feel the Holy Spirit in your life. The Holy Spirit will guide and protect you. He will help you to pray to the Father in heaven.

Prayer: Mary, I want the Holy Spirit to come to me!

DAY 20

You must know that when you "Hail" Mary, she immediately greets you! – St. Bernadine of Siena

Do you know what Mary's favorite prayer is? The Rosary! Every time you pray a Hail Mary in the Rosary, you give Mary a rose in heaven. The Rosary helps you pray about Jesus' life. You can imagine how he was born, baptized, died on the cross, and even rose from the dead. All of these events are called the Mysteries of the Rosary.

Prayer: Mary, I want to give you lots of roses in heaven!

DAY 21

The Holy Rosary is a powerful weapon. Use it with confidence and you'll be amazed at the results. — St. Josemaria Escriva

As you pray the Rosary, be sure to bring lots of prayer intentions to Mary. What would you like Mary to pray for? Who needs her prayers? Plus, because she is Jesus' mother, she will bring your prayer intentions right to her Son. Furthermore, because she is the Queen of Heaven, she will make your prayers even more beautiful and important to Jesus.

Prayer: Mary, bring my prayers to your Son, Jesus!

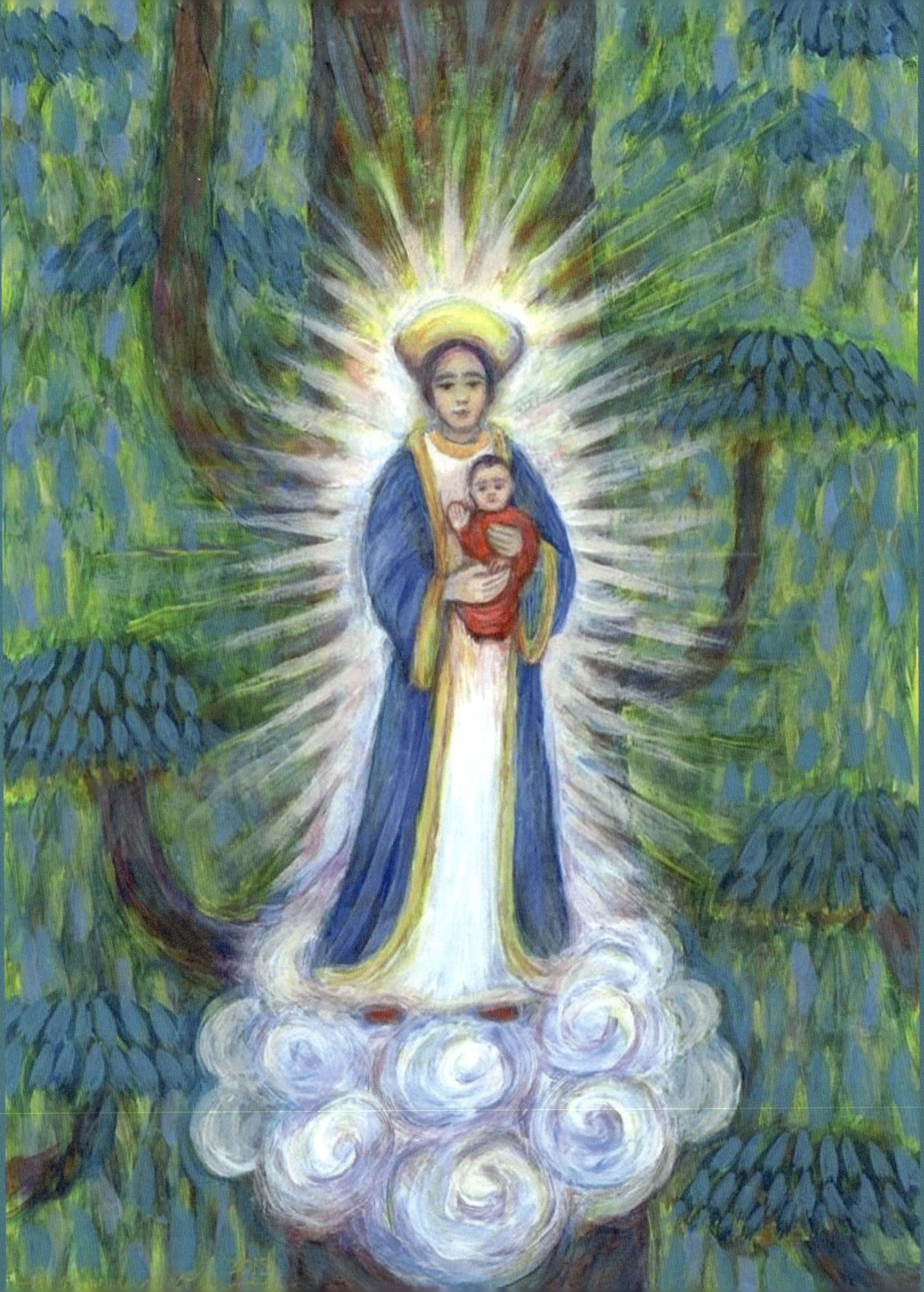

Day 22

Do not be ashamed to recite the Rosary alone. While you walk along the streets to school, to the university, or to work, or as you commute by public transport. – St. John Paul II

Remember how I said that Mary has a special mission for you? Here is a hint about your mission. Part of your mission will be praying the Rosary. Mary does great and wonderful things through the Rosary. But she needs people like you to pray. You may be little, but your prayers are great!

Prayer: Mary, use the rosaries I pray for great things!

Day 23

Was she beautiful?
"Oh! Oh! Yes indeed! And even more than that! So lovely that, when you have seen her once, you would willingly die to see her again!" – St. Bernadette

Did you know that Mary has come down from heaven to appear to people? These visions are called apparitions. What would it be like if Mary visited you? She has visited children before, like St. Bernadette at Lourdes. She had a special mission for those children, just like she has for you.

Prayer: Mary, thank you for visiting from heaven!

DAY 24

When you pray the Rosary, say after each mystery: "O my Jesus..."
- Our Lady of Fatima

Mary came from heaven to visit three shepherd children in a place called Fatima. She told them many things about heaven and hell. She also taught them special prayers. One prayer, the "Oh My Jesus" prayer, is to be prayed after each mystery in the Rosary.

O my Jesus, forgive us our sins,
save us from the fires of Hell. Lead all souls to Heaven,
especially those who are most in need of thy mercy.

Prayer: Mary, help me to learn your special Rosary prayer.

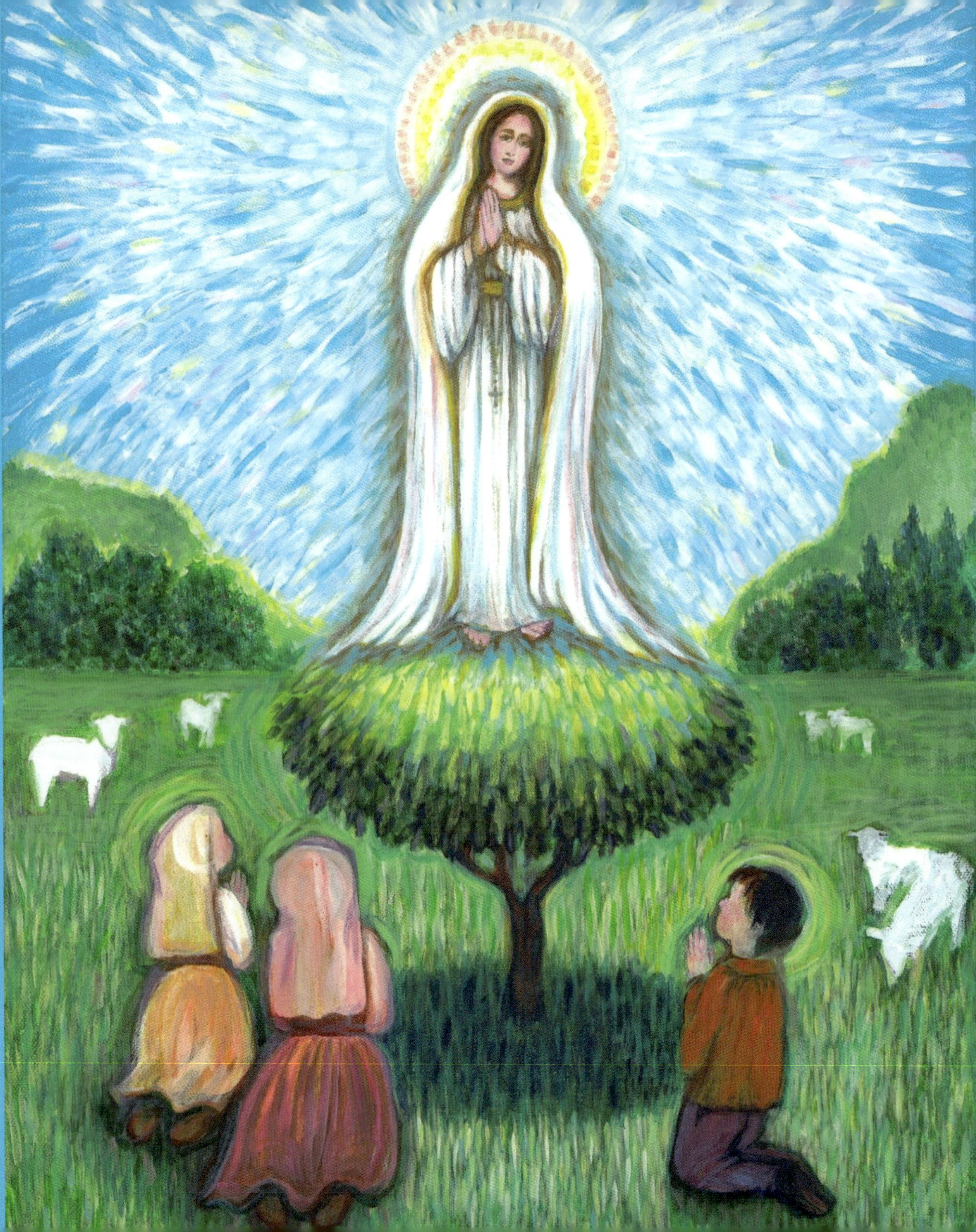

DAY 25

The greatest saints will also be the most diligent in praying to the most blessed Virgin. – St. Louis de Montfort

When Mary visited Fatima, the children asked her if they were going to heaven someday. When the little boy, Francisco, asked her, she said that he must first pray many rosaries. Would you like to go to heaven someday? A sure way to heaven is to stay very close to Mary and to pray her Rosary every day.

Prayer: Mary, I want to pray a Rosary every day!

DAY 26

Do you love my Son? Do you love me?
Then sacrifice yourself for me. — Our Lady at Beauraing

Besides praying the Rosary every day, I will tell you another part of the mission Mary has for you. She wants you to offer many sacrifices. What is a sacrifice? A sacrifice is doing a good and loving act because it is what God wants you to do, even though it is sometimes difficult. These acts can be offered as sacrifices to God.

Prayer: Mary, please teach me how to offer sacrifices to you!

Day 27

Will you offer yourselves to God, and bear all the sufferings He sends you? In reparation for all the sins that offend Him? And for the conversion of sinners? – Our Lady of Fatima

Do you know who St. Therese is? She's a great saint in heaven now, but once she was little just like you and was able to make little sacrifices. She knew that she could offer lots of sacrifices to God, like making her bed, sharing with her sisters, and deciding not to cry when she was mad. These were all wonderful sacrifices to offer to God!

Prayer: Mary, I have lots of little sacrifices to offer you!

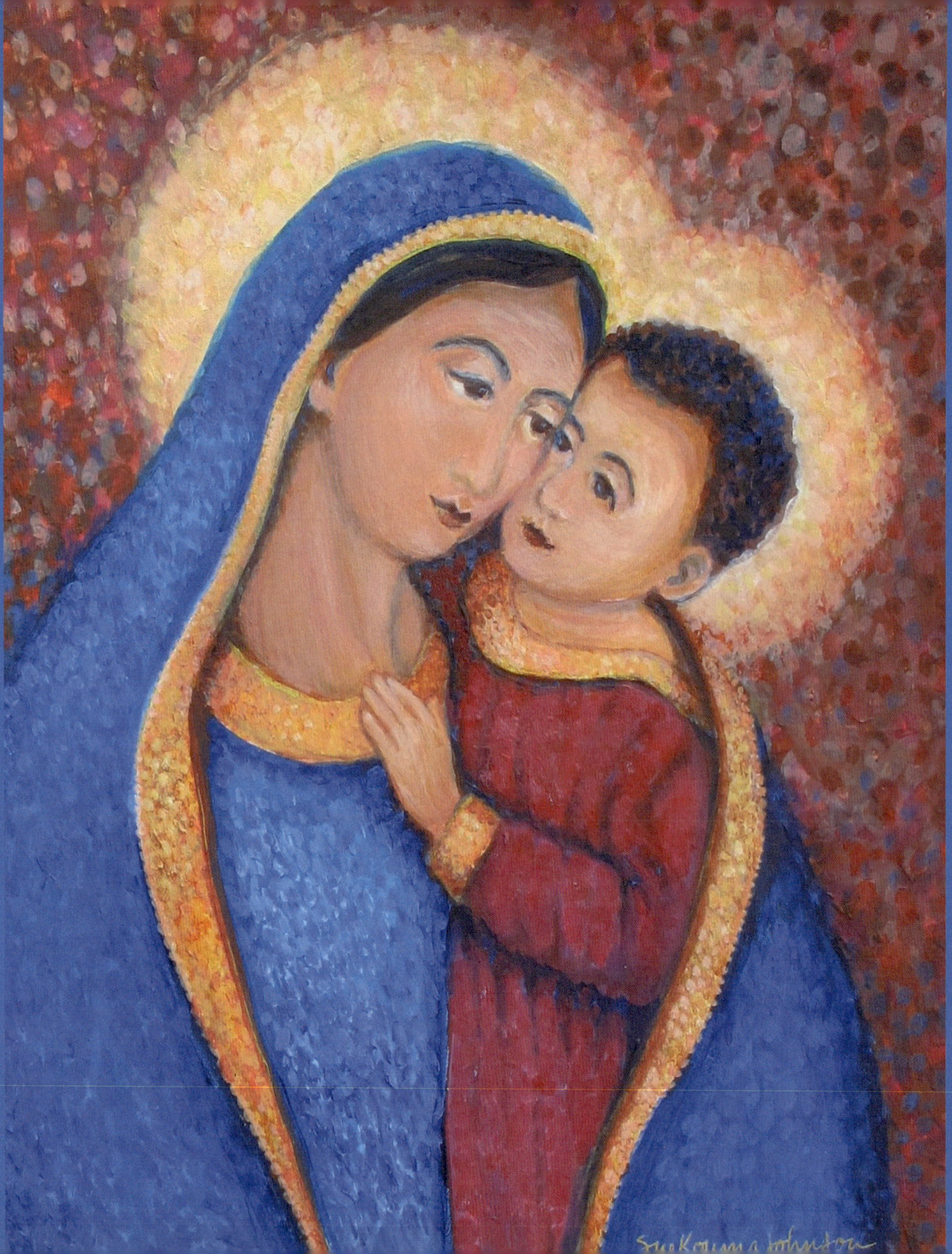

DAY 28

Sacrifice yourself for sinners and pray many times, especially whenever you make some sacrifice. – Our Lady of Fatima

Just like the special Rosary prayer that Mary gave the children of Fatima, Mary also gave them a special prayer for when they are offering sacrifices. This prayer will help you to remember that your sacrifices are helping people to come to know Jesus and Mary.

O Jesus, this is for love of Thee, in reparation for sins committed against the Immaculate Heart of Mary and the conversion of poor sinners.

Prayer: Mary, help me to remember this special sacrifice prayer!

Day 29

*Let us run to Mary, and as her little children,
cast ourselves into her arms with a perfect confidence.
– St. Francis de Sales*

Today I am going to tell you the final part of your mission for Mary. Besides praying the Rosary and offering sacrifices every day, your mission includes choosing to pledge your life to Mary. You do this by praying a special prayer called a Consecration Prayer. This prayer will show Mary that you want her to be your heavenly mother and queen.

Prayer: Mary, I want to consecrate myself to you!

Day 30

Jesus wishes to make use of you to make me known and loved.
— Our Lady of Fatima

You have learned that praying the Rosary, offering sacrifices, and saying a special consecration prayer every day is your mission. But why? Because these three actions will help Mary's Immaculate Heart triumph, which means that she will win many hearts for God! What is Mary's Immaculate Heart? Her heart is where all of her love for her Son, Jesus, is kept.

Prayer: Mary, I want to learn more about your Immaculate Heart!

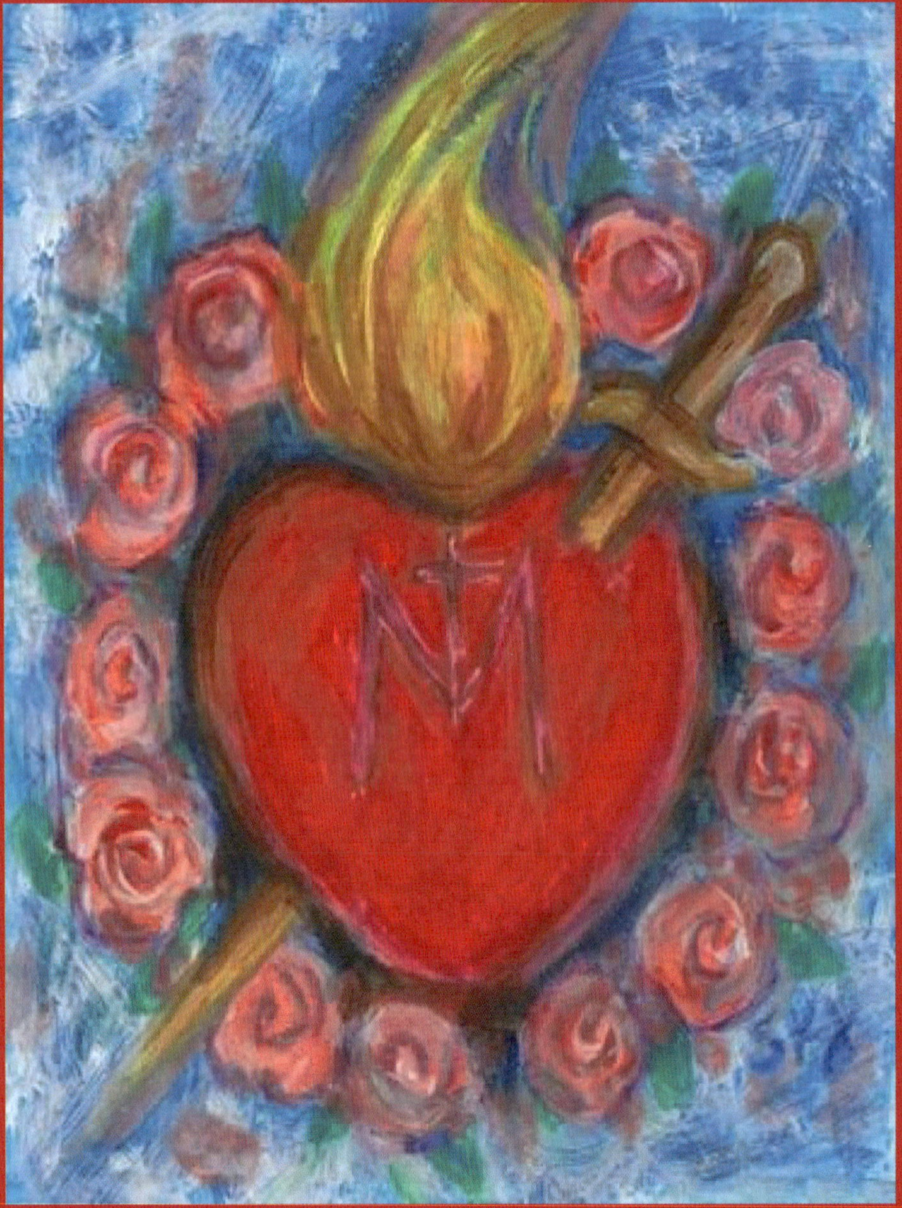

DAY 31

In the end, my Immaculate Heart will triumph.
– Our Lady of Fatima

Mary's heart is very great and powerful. Throughout her life, Mary thought about God's gifts in her heart. All of the joyful, luminous, sorrowful, and glorious times of Jesus' life are kept in Mary's Immaculate Heart. How happy her heart was at his birth and excited as Jesus worked his first miracles. Her heart suffered as Jesus was dying and rejoiced when Jesus rose from the dead.

Prayer: Mary, your Immaculate Heart is so great!

DAY 32

If what I say to you is true, many souls will be saved and there will be peace. – Our Lady of Fatima

If you accept this mission from Mary, which will help her heart to triumph, many people will be brought to God. Mary wants our Faith in God to be very great. You may be little, but by praying the Rosary, offering sacrifices, and praying your special consecration prayer every day, you can help many people be brought to God. She wants people to pray to God and serve Him.

Prayer: Mary, I want to bring many people to know God!

Day 33

Be good and resigned to the will of God. Pray often, especially the Rosary. Now, farewell, my children, until we meet in Heaven.
– Our Lady of Heede

Your mission begins tomorrow. You will say a consecration prayer to accept your special mission from Mary. You must not take this mission lightly. Mary, the Queen of Heaven and Earth needs you to commit to your mission in order to help you and others love God and do His Holy Will. With your help, Mary's Immaculate Heart will triumph!

Prayer: Mary, may your Immaculate Heart triumph!

Consecration Day

Congratulations! Your consecration day is here! Be sure to pray your consecration prayer found on the next page. Also, here are some ideas of how to make your day extra special.

Thank you for answering Mary's call!

- Go to Mass and confession
- Put flowers by a Mary statue
- Light a votive candle
- Create a Rosary
- Distribute rosaries
- Create a Marian shrine
- Watch a movie about Mary
- Create a play about Mary's life
- Color or draw a picture of Mary
- Pray a Rosary at a nursing home
- Sing Marian songs
- Plant a Mary garden
- Plan a Mary tea party
- Pray the Litany of Mary

Consecration Prayer

Mary, Queen of Heaven and Earth,

I accept your mission for me. I will give my life to you and your Son, Jesus. Every day I will choose to offer sacrifices and pray to you. I know that I am little, but I believe that I have been given a great mission by you to bring many people to God.

May your Immaculate Heart Triumph!

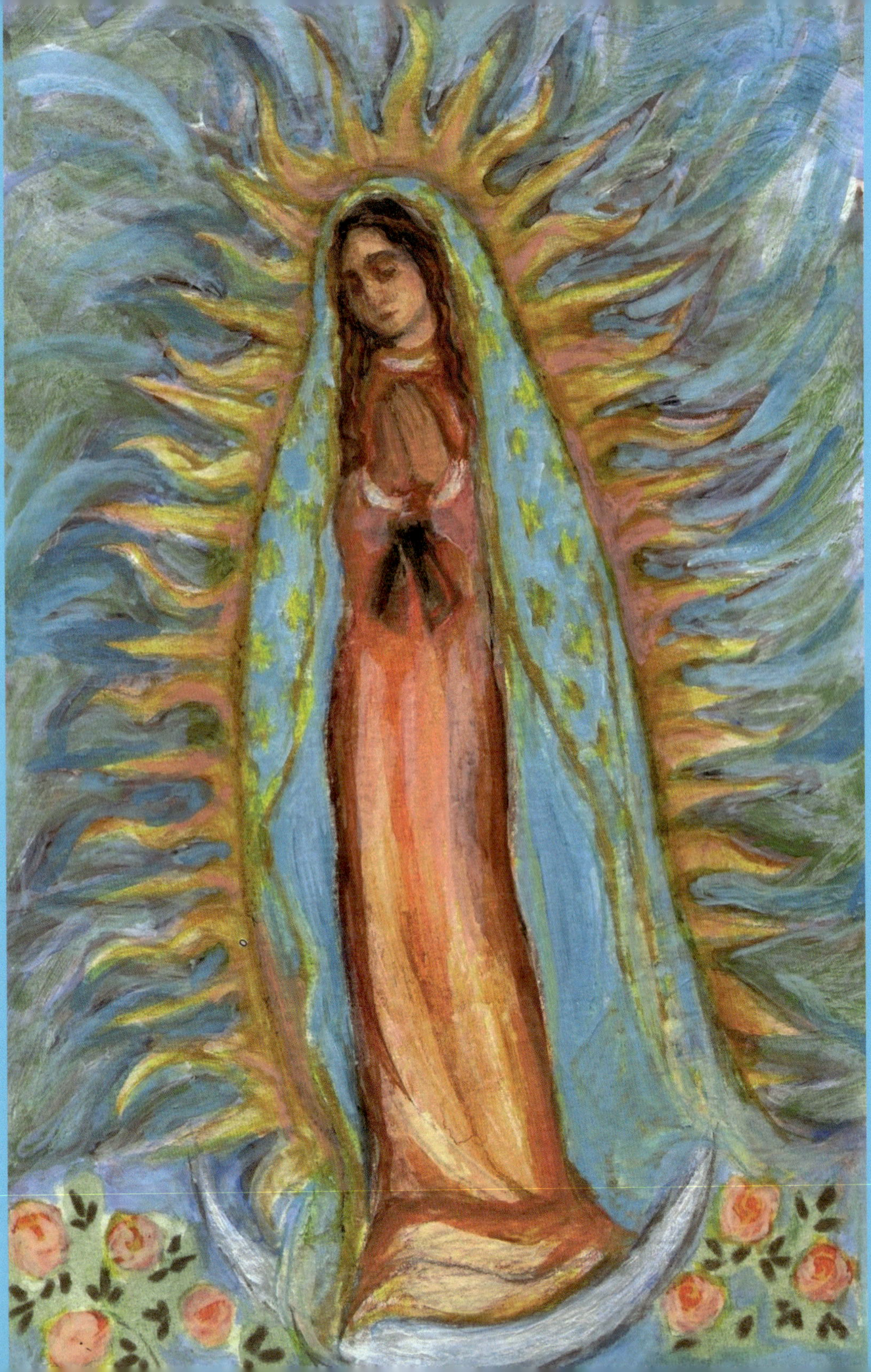

After your Consecration

Praying your consecration prayer is only the beginning in fulfilling your mission for Mary. Take time every day to say the daily consecration prayer found below. Also, pray the Rosary and offer sacrifices to God. You can help Mary's Immaculate Heart triumph!

Daily Consecration Prayer:

Jesus, I offer my day to you!

Mary, I consecrate myself to you!

Collect All the My Little Nazareth Books

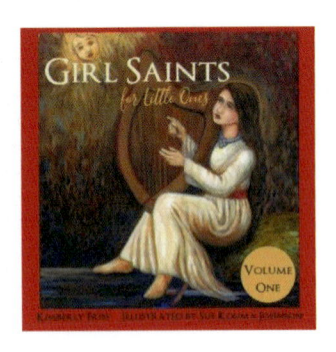

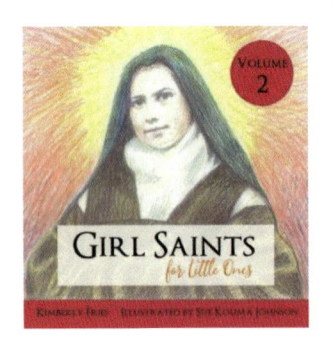

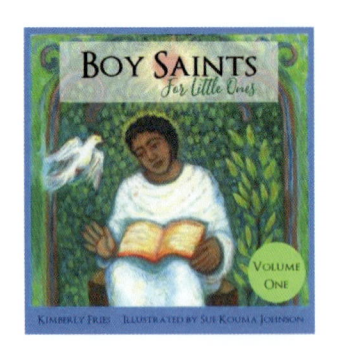

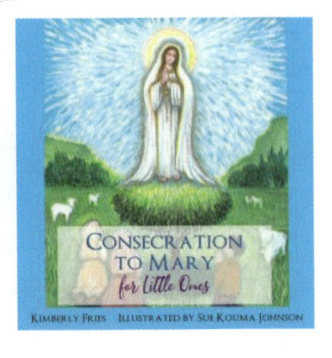

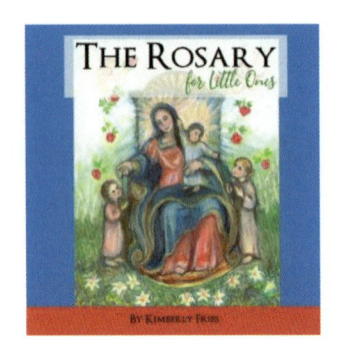

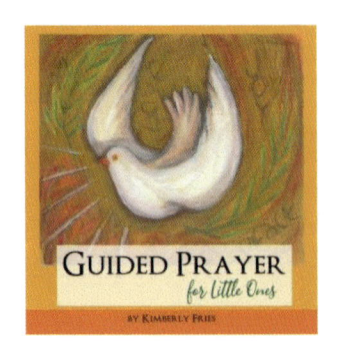

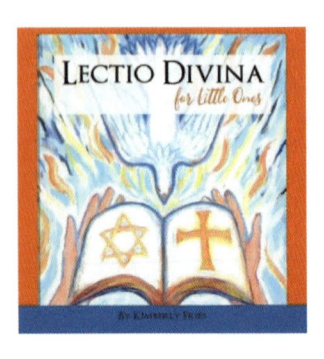

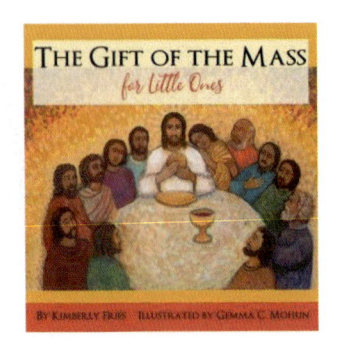

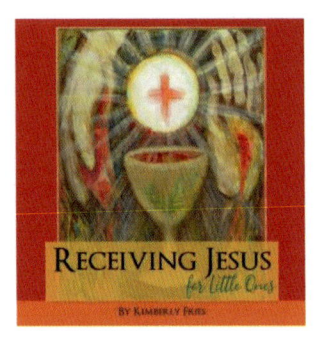

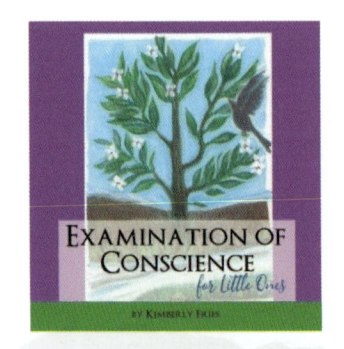

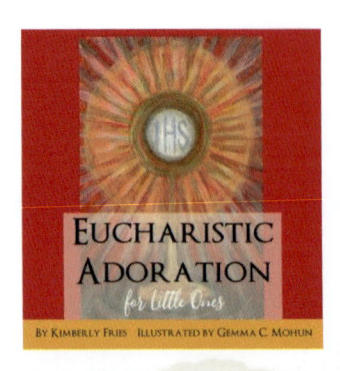

- Girl Saints for Little Ones, Volume One
- Girl Saints for Little Ones, Volume 2
- Boy Saints for Little Ones, Volume One
- Divine Mercy for Little Ones
- Consecration to Mary for Little Ones
- The Rosary for Little Ones
- Guided Prayer for Little Ones
- Lectio Divina for Little Ones
- The Gift of the Mass for Little Ones
- Receiving Jesus for Little Ones
- Examination of Conscience for Little Ones
- Eucharistic Adoration for Little Ones

Meet the Author

I'm Kimberly Fries, mom and author. I live in South Dakota with my husband and three children. Creating Catholic books to help children develop a personal relationship with God, Mary, and the saints has been such a joy for me. I pray that my books greatly bless your family and assist you in your journey to become saints!

Meet the Illustrator

Sue Kouma Johnson lives in Nebraska with her husband. After earning her BFA, she devoted her time to raising five children. Now she has taken up her calling as a Catholic artist, painting saints and images that express her love for her Catholic Faith.

See more of her artwork: www.catholicartandjewelry.com

Visit her Etsy shop: www.etsy.com/shop/TreeOfHeaven

I would love to hear from you!

Please write a review at Amazon.com.

Want to be the first to know about my new releases?
Follow me on Facebook, Instagram, Youtube, and my blog!

Interested in getting wholesale, group, and parish prices?
E-mail me at mylittlenazareth@gmail.com

www.mylittlenazareth.com

Printed in Germany
by Amazon Distribution
GmbH, Leipzig